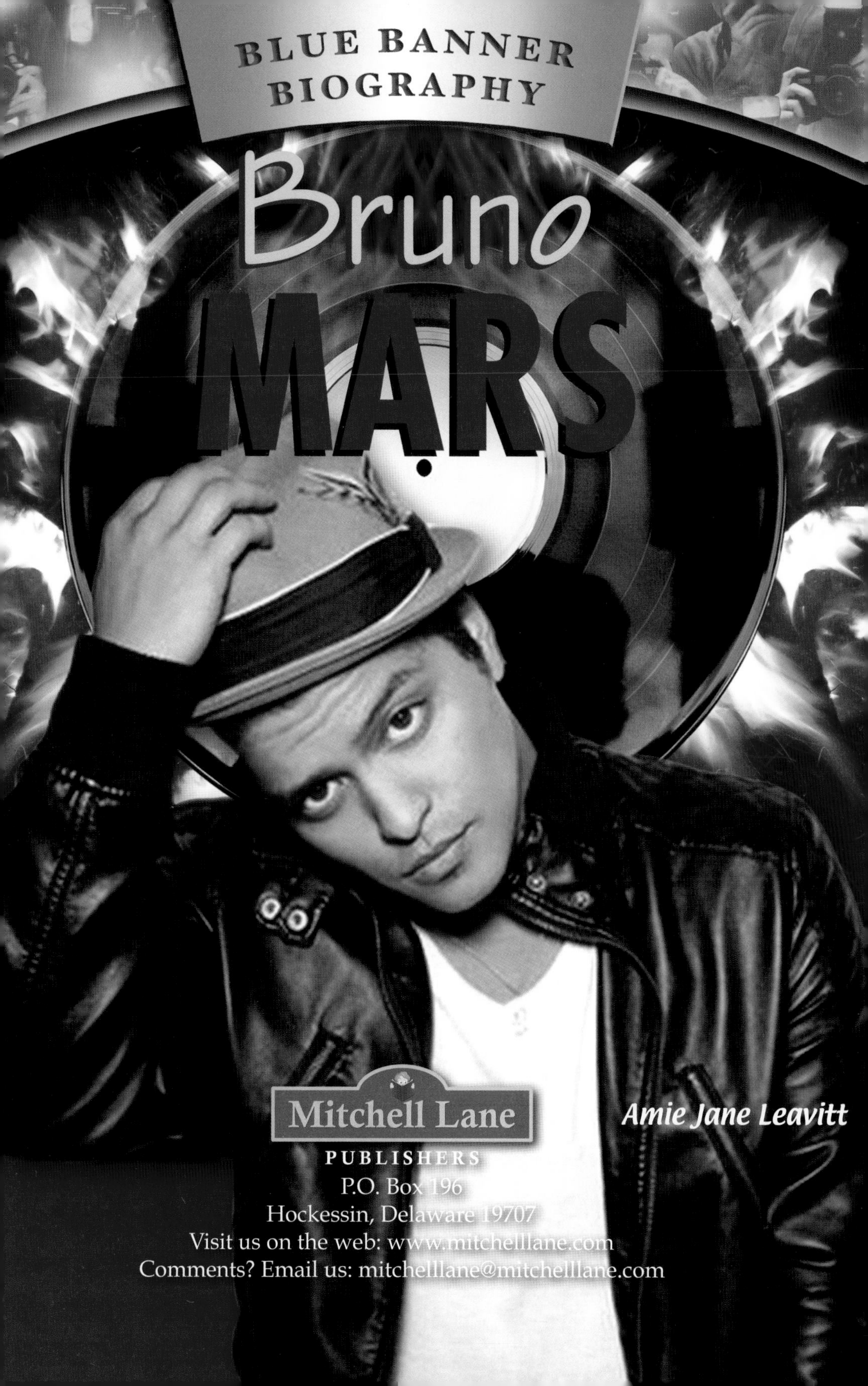

BLUE BANNER
BIOGRAPHY

Bruno MARS

Mitchell Lane
PUBLISHERS
P.O. Box 196
Hockessin, Delaware 19707
Visit us on the web: www.mitchelllane.com
Comments? Email us: mitchelllane@mitchelllane.com

Amie Jane Leavitt

Mitchell Lane
PUBLISHERS

Printing   1   2   3   4   5   6   7   8   9

Blue Banner Biographies

Adele	Ice Cube	Miguel Tejada
Alicia Keys	Ja Rule	Nancy Pelosi
Allen Iverson	Jamie Foxx	Natasha Bedingfield
Ashanti	Jay-Z	One Direction
Ashlee Simpson	Jennifer Hudson	Orianthi
Ashton Kutcher	Jennifer Lopez	Orlando Bloom
Avril Lavigne	Jessica Simpson	P. Diddy
Blake Lively	J. K. Rowling	Peyton Manning
Bow Wow	Joe Flacco	Pink
Brett Favre	John Legend	Prince William
Britney Spears	Justin Berfield	Queen Latifah
Bruno Mars	Justin Timberlake	Rihanna
CC Sabathia	Kanye West	Robert Downey Jr.
Carrie Underwood	Kate Hudson	Robert Pattinson
Chris Brown	Katy Perry	Ron Howard
Chris Daughtry	Keith Urban	Sean Kingston
Christina Aguilera	Kelly Clarkson	Selena
Ciara	Kenny Chesney	Shakira
Clay Aiken	Ke$ha	Shia LaBeouf
Cole Hamels	Kristen Stewart	Shontelle Layne
Condoleezza Rice	Lady Gaga	Soulja Boy Tell 'Em
Corbin Bleu	Lance Armstrong	Stephenie Meyer
Daniel Radcliffe	Leona Lewis	Taylor Swift
David Ortiz	Lil Wayne	T.I.
David Wright	Lindsay Lohan	Timbaland
Derek Jeter	Ludacris	Tim McGraw
Drew Brees	Mariah Carey	Tim Tebow
Eminem	Mario	Toby Keith
Eve	Mary J. Blige	Usher
Fergie	Mary-Kate and Ashley Olsen	Vanessa Anne Hudgens
Flo Rida	Megan Fox	Will.i.am
Gwen Stefani		Zac Efron

Library of Congress Cataloging-in-Publication Data
Leavitt, Amie Jane.
  Bruno Mars / by Amie Jane Leavitt.
     p. cm. — (Blue banner biographies)
  Includes bibliographical references and index.
  ISBN 978-1-61228-316-6 (library bound)
  1. Mars, Bruno, 1985– — Juvenile literature. 2. Musicians — United States — Biography — Juvenile literature. I. Title.
  ML3930.M318L43 2013
  782.42164092 — dc23
  [B]
                                                                                              2012018302
eBook ISBN: 9781612283876

ABOUT THE AUTHOR: Amie Jane Leavitt is an accomplished author and photographer. She graduated from Brigham Young University as an education major and has since taught all subjects and grade levels in both private and public schools. She has written dozens of books for kids, has contributed to online and print media, and has worked as a consultant, writer, and editor for numerous educational publishing and assessment companies. While in college, Amie lived on Oahu—the same island that Bruno Mars calls home. With her great love for the people, history, and culture of the Hawaiian islands, Amie particularly enjoyed writing about Bruno Mars.

PUBLISHER'S NOTE: The following story has been thoroughly researched, and to the best of our knowledge represents a true story. While every possible effort has been made to ensure accuracy, the publisher will not assume liability for damages caused by inaccuracies in the data and makes no warranty on the accuracy of the information contained herein. This story has not been authorized or endorsed by Bruno Mars.

Blue Banner Biography

Bruno Mars is fast becoming a worldwide sensation. Here, he jams out with his band at the MTV Europe Music Awards in Belfast, Northern Ireland.

CHAPTER 1

Coming Home

An eerie quiet fills the sold-out Honolulu Neal S. Blaisdell Arena as a man in blue jeans and black T-shirt walks up to the center microphone and begins to speak. "Now therefore I, Peter B. Carlisle, thirteenth mayor of the City and County of Honolulu, do hereby proclaim December 19, 2010, to be BRUNO MARS DAY!" As he says the last three words, he throws his hands up into the air and the crowd goes wild. The once quiet arena is now filled with a sea of cheers, screams, and applause.

The arena's darkness is replaced by a single spotlight illuminating the center of the stage. There, standing in the light are six men donned in white shirts, black pants, black skinny ties and sky-blue sport jackets. The man in the center is none other than Bruno Mars.

"Bruno, Bruno, Bruno, Bruno, Bruno, Bruno!" the crowd chants.

"How's it?" he asks the crowd using a typical Hawaiian slang phrase. "Happy Bruno Mars Day!" he jokes.

The crowd responds with raucous applause.

"Yo, Hawaii," he yells into the mic. "I'm home!"

Just a few years before, Bruno had been in L.A. struggling. He was broke and trying to figure out what to do. He didn't want to come back to Hawaii as a failure.

And now, it was clear that he hadn't. Bruno had only recently flown back into the Honolulu International Airport. Today he was playing a concert to 10,000 screaming fans at the city's largest arena. It hardly seemed possible that it was true. But it was!

"Bruno, Bruno, Bruno, Bruno, Bruno, Bruno!" the crowd chants. *"How's it?"* he asks the crowd . . . *"Happy Bruno Mars Day!"* he jokes.

While the band was staying on Oahu, Bruno drove them around in his old high school car: a green Jeep Cherokee. "My mom never sold it," Bruno explains on his video documentary for the trip, called "Bruno Comes Home." "Why rent a car when you got one?" He drove them through the streets of Waikiki showing them the places he used to work as a kid and a teen. They stopped at some of his favorite local places to eat: traditional plate lunches at Zippy's and Rainbow Drive-In and Korean food at Sorabol. They also spent some time hanging out at some of Bruno's favorite island spots like Sandy Beach on the southeast corner of the island.

Two days later, the band performed for fans at The Castle Theater on the island of Maui. This time, they were wearing Aloha shirts and orchid leis. "If you're ever going to play a show rockin' Aloha shirts," he explains on the documentary, "It's got to be in Hawaii." During the concert, Bruno played the ukulele in some of his numbers and the guitar in others. Both he and his fellow bandmember and business partner Phillip Lawrence jumped around on stage as they sang the music. Everyone in the audience could feel the group's energy.

Bruno's concerts are different from other shows and he explains why in his video documentary. "It's all about putting on a show," he says. "I think the best part of our show is that you can tell we're all friends up there . . . That's where the magic happens—when you see the interaction between the band . . . We go up there and genuinely have the time of our life."

Being on stage just feels natural to Bruno, like being at home. And it should. Ever since Bruno was a young kid, he has been performing on stage. It's what he has always wanted and it's what he lives for now. "Performing from such a young age just got me so comfortable on stage," Bruno told *MidWeek*'s Melissa Moniz in 2010. Besides the recording studio, the only other place he would rather be is on the stage performing for his fans. He explains why music is so important to him and to his family. "Everyone in my family sings, plays instruments. It's what we do," he says.

Bruno has been an entertainer ever since he was a small child. He came from a family of entertainers and he wanted to be just like them. He particularly loved performing Elvis songs on stage.

CHAPTER 2

Little Elvis

Days and weeks in the warm, tropical paradise of Honolulu, Hawaii can easily blend into one with each day as beautiful as the next. But October 8, 1985 wasn't just another day for Pete and Bernadette "Bernie" Hernandez. This was the day that their second son was born. They named him Peter Gene Hernandez.

When Peter was still a toddler, his father started calling him Bruno. "My dad was a fan of the wrestler Bruno Sammartino, who was heavyset," Bruno told a reporter for the *New York Daily News*. "When I was a kid I was a little pudgy. I reminded him of a wrestler." The nickname stuck and Peter was called Bruno by friends and family from that point on. Only his teachers at school continued to call him Peter. In his late teens, he added "Mars" to his name because "A lot of girls say I'm out of this world," he told the *Asian Journal*. "So I was like I guess I'm from Mars."

Bruno has often said that music is just in the air in Hawaii. It's almost as if you can hear it coming from the flowers, trees, and ocean. It most definitely was in the air in the Hernandez home. Pete and Bernie met at a hula show —

he was a Latin percussionist and she was a hula dancer. After their marriage, they continued to perform in their own family show with their brothers and eventually their two boys and four girls: Eric, Jamie Kailani, Bruno, Tahiti, Tiara, and Presley. They called their group the "Lovenotes." It was a 1950s doo-wop Vegas-style show at the Sheraton Waikiki. They did performances where they pretended to be other famous singers from the 1950s and 1960s. Chuck Berry, Jerry Lee Lewis, Little Richard, and Elvis Presley were some of their favorite people to impersonate. Pete's Puerto Rican and Brooklyn upbringing combined with Bernie's Filipina heritage brought a unique style to the stage. It wasn't long before the Lovenotes became one of Hawaii's most popular oldies groups.

Bruno has often said that music is just in the air in Hawaii. It's almost as if you can hear it coming from the flowers, trees, and ocean.

It could be said that Bruno was born with music running through his veins. From the moment he could walk, he wanted to be on stage with his family. In 2011, Bruno's family members explained to the *Honolulu Star Advertiser* what Bruno was like as a kid. "At every family gathering all of us would be singing," recalls Bruno's uncle, John Valentine, "and he would be the biggest ham." His mother says that the rest of her children were shy, but not Bruno. "You put them on stage and they choke, but Bruno wanted to be on stage."

Baby Bruno, still in diapers, was already putting together his own act at home. He knew how to work the VCR and would fast-forward and rewind tapes until they landed on his favorite parts: the Elvis numbers. He would watch these acts over and over again. Then, he'd go to his room and rehearse until he got his act down perfectly. When people would come over, he'd perform for them. "Even if he couldn't pronounce the words, he would sing the beat and he was on pitch," his mother told the *Honolulu Star Advertiser*.

Every time his family would go out on stage and perform, Bruno longed to be with them. "Yeah, from a very young age I remember watching the show and being completely fascinated," Bruno told *Blues & Soul* reporter, Pete Lewis. He would watch his uncle play guitar and do his Elvis routine. He'd see his dad conducting everyone and directing the show. He'd listen to his mom sing with her beautiful voice. He begged his dad to let him be part of the act, and after much pleading on Bruno's part, his father finally agreed.

Bruno's first time on stage with the family was while they were performing at a hotel opening celebration in Japan. Four-year-old Bruno walked out on stage. Then, he started performing one of the Elvis routines that he had been practicing for two years at home. "He started shaking his legs [like Elvis] and the people went wild," his father told the *Honolulu Star Advertiser*. On that day, the Hernandez family knew they had a little star on their hands. "Ever since that moment, I've been addicted," Bruno admits on his official website.

> *It could be said that Bruno was born with music running through his veins.*

Little Bruno

After that, Bruno became a regular part of the family's show, performing every night of the week. He was known as the world's smallest Elvis impersonator, or "Little Elvis." Word about this little performer soon got out to the media. He was featured on the cover of Hawaii's *MidWeek* magazine in 1990 with a bold headline that read "Elvis Lives!" This caught the eye of Hollywood and in 1992 he was flown to Los Angeles to portray a "mini Elvis" in the Nicolas Cage film *Honeymoon in Vegas.*

The School Boys

Bruno continued impersonating Elvis until he was fourteen. That's when he started his Michael Jackson routine in his family's "Legends in Concert" show. He dressed up in replicas of Jackson's funky getups from the 1970s and 1980s and sang some of Jackson's most famous songs while he danced on stage.

During Bruno's childhood and teenage years, he learned how to play a variety of instruments without having any lessons. Since he came from a musical family, there were always musical instruments like a drum set, piano, guitars, and ukuleles at his house. So, he'd just sit down with the instrument and learn how to play it. "That's just how I learned," Bruno told *Hawaii News Now,* "by just being surrounded by it my whole life." His mom calls her son a prodigy, or a person who has exceptional talents. After all, how many people can pick up instruments they've never played and just teach themselves how to play them? By age 18, Bruno could play the piano, guitar, bass, harmonica, and congas.

Bruno loved music more than anything else, and he didn't let anything else get in his way. His father told the *Honolulu Star Advertiser*, "I'd rarely see him carrying books, but he always had a guitar or a ukulele or something."

While attending President Theodore Roosevelt High School in Honolulu, Bruno joined a singing group with three of his friends: Joey Kaalekahi, Dwayne Andres and Reid Kobashigawa. The four classmates decided to call their group "The School Boys," since after all, that's what they

Bruno's talents as a musician don't just include singing. He plays many instruments, and writes music, too.

were. The group began performing with the Lovenotes at Waikiki's Ilikai Hotel. They mainly performed classic songs by Motown artists like The Temptations and The Isley Brothers which complemented the Lovenotes' oldies theme. But the teens wanted to add contemporary numbers to their repertoire too. They were fans of *NSYNC and the Backstreet Boys.

One night after a particularly great concert, the group was feeling really amped up. As they drove through the streets of Waikiki, they noticed two girls waiting at a the drive-thru of a fast food restaurant. Even though it was raining, The School Boys hopped out of their car and started serenading the girls. "We'd had a great show that night and we were ready for anything. We saw those two girls and something had to happen," Bruno told a reporter for the *Honolulu Star-Bulletin* in 2000. The girls were so impressed that they started attending some of The School Boys' performances at the Ilikai. "Girls love it when you croon to them," Bruno later told *Village Voice.*

In addition to singing five nights a week at the Ilikai, Bruno also helped out in his school's fine arts department. One year, he directed a school play, and several times during his high school years, he choreographed the school's pep rallies.

Since Bruno grew up on one of the most beautiful islands on earth, he took advantage of typical island activities. Music had always been his focus, so he never had time to become a really good surfer. But he did like to ride the waves on boogie boards and then relax on the sand building sandcastles and hanging out with his friends. He also loved his mom's and grandma's homemade cooking. Their chicken adobo and Spanish rice were two of his favorites.

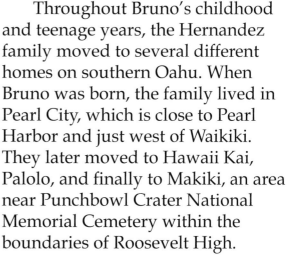

Since Bruno grew up on one of the most beautiful islands on earth, he took advantage of typical island activities.

Throughout Bruno's childhood and teenage years, the Hernandez family moved to several different homes on southern Oahu. When Bruno was born, the family lived in Pearl City, which is close to Pearl Harbor and just west of Waikiki. They later moved to Hawaii Kai, Palolo, and finally to Makiki, an area near Punchbowl Crater National Memorial Cemetery within the boundaries of Roosevelt High.

When Bruno graduated from Roosevelt High School at age 17 in 2003, he decided to leave his beautiful island of Oahu and head to Los Angeles. He just didn't want to be a performer singing other people's music anymore. He wanted to be a musician and an artist. His sister Jamie Kailani had already moved there a few years before and had connections in the music industry. She felt that she could help Bruno at least get an audition. So, he bought a one-way ticket, boarded a jet at Honolulu International Airport, and set off for his brand new life in L.A. He planned on returning someday, but he hoped he would be able to return as a big star.

CHAPTER 4

Moving to Tinsel Town

Bruno was excited about moving to Los Angeles. After all, in his mind, that's where all his dreams were going to come true. Yet, things didn't turn out exactly as he had planned. Although he was signed quickly by Universal Motown in 2004, nothing really happened after that. He waited for the record label to tell him what to do and for big producers to invite him to come to the studio and record for them, but no one did. He thought it was going to be like the movies, but as he told *Entertainment Weekly* in 2010, he soon found out that "it's not like you sign a record contract and then you're rubbing shoulders with Timbaland and Pharrell."

A year after signing Bruno as one of its recording artists, Motown released him from his contract. Bruno takes responsibility for the label's decision, saying that he may have been too young. "I don't think I was ready," he told *Blues & Soul's* Pete Lewis. He had never really recorded before and he certainly had never written a song. He had always been too busy performing other people's music. As would be expected, this was a very discouraging time for Bruno. Here, he thought he had it made it when he landed a recording contract so quickly after moving to L.A., and now he was back at square one. For the first time, he struggled to pay his rent. His phone was even being shut off because he didn't have the money to pay the bill. He tried to make money as a DJ, but that didn't last because he didn't have any experience as a DJ. "I lost that job pretty quick," he told Brad Wete with *Entertainment Weekly*.

> **As Bruno and Phillip started working together more and more, Bruno realized that he really did have a talent for songwriting.**

At one point, he got really frustrated with how much harder things were in L.A. than he had imagined. He missed his friends and family. He missed home. He missed Hawaii. L.A. had a fast-paced lifestyle and he was used to the laid-back island life of Oahu. He seriously considered quitting and going home. That's when his uncle John Valentine jumped in with words of encouragement. He told him that he just had to stay and keep trying; he couldn't quit, yet. Bruno had always respected his uncle's advice. After all, it was John who had encouraged him to come to L.A. in the first place. So, he agreed to stay a little longer. And luckily for him, and the entire music world, he did. Just a short time later, he met his soon-to-be business partner and best friend, songwriter Phillip Lawrence.

Phillip and Bruno clicked immediately. "Working with Bruno is like hanging out with my homie," Phillip Lawrence told *USA TODAY*. As Bruno and Phillip started working together more and more, Bruno realized that he really did have a talent for songwriting.

At first, he wrote songs with the intention of singing them himself. But then, a record producer asked him if he would sell one of his songs for the boy band Menudo to sing. "At first I was like, no way! This is my work. This is my art!" Bruno told *Entertainment Weekly's* Brad Wete. He wanted to perform his music, not let someone else do it. But when the record producer offered him $20,000 for the song, Bruno couldn't refuse. "It was either that, or I was going back to Hawaii," Bruno told *Billboard's* Jason Lipshutz. It was at that moment that Phillip and Bruno decided that writing songs for other artists wasn't such a bad idea—at least temporarily. "We put the artist stuff on the back burner and took some of the pressure off ourselves," Bruno recalls.

Phillip and Bruno, along with their sound engineer friend Ari Levine, decided to start their own songwriting and production team. They called themselves "The Smeezingtons." The name might sound a little unusual, but

Bruno enjoys working with his business partners Phillip Lawrence (left) and Ari Levine (center). Collectively the trio is known as The Smeezingtons. They are all very good friends.

Bruno loves it because he says it shows that they don't take themselves too seriously. "We used to always say in the studio, 'Yo, this is going to be a smash!' And then it turned into, 'This is a smeeze!' Then, 'This is a Smeezington,'" he told *Entertainment Weekly*.

Bruno liked writing and producing, but he had certainly never envisioned that things would work out for him this way.

The Smeezingtons started writing songs for all sorts of artists and found tremendous success in the process. Phillip Lawrence credits their ability to do that to the fact that they both came from musical families. "Our inspiration is kind of all over the place," Phillip told ASCAP.com, "but I think it really helps us as songwriters to understand how to capture an authentic sound for many different genres." The Smeezingtons do indeed write for a wide variety of musical genres. They wrote "Right Round" for rapper Flo Rida which was their first song to hit Number One on *Billboard's* Hot 100. They also wrote "Long Distance" for R&B singer Brandy, and "Wavin' Flag" for K'Naan, which became the theme song for the 2010 World Cup.

In addition to those artists, The Smeezingtons have also written and produced for Sean Kingston, Far*East Movement, Kid Cudi, Snoop Dogg, Lil Wayne, Bad Meets Evil, Cee-Lo Green, Travie McCoy, B.o.B, Matisyahu, and a variety of others.

Bruno liked writing and producing, but he had certainly never envisioned that things would work out for him this way. "I never moved to California to be a producer or a

Bruno's ability to sing a variety of musical genres has allowed him to write music for and perform with a wide range of musicians. Here he sings with rapper B.o.B during the Grammy Nominations Concert in Los Angeles in 2010.

songwriter. It just fell into place. For some reason, it took me to this left turn, that I just had to ride out until people started noticing it's me writing the song," Bruno told Malika Dudley, a reporter with *Hawaii News Now*.

CHAPTER 5

He's Out of This World

*I*n 2009, Aaron Bay-Schuck, a producer at Atlantic Records, noticed The Smeezingtons' writing credit on "Right Round." He contacted Bruno and made arrangements for the team to come in and meet the co-presidents of Elektra Records, a division of Atlantic Records. Bruno played five songs for them including "Nothin' on You" and "Billionaire." The Elektra executives were immediately impressed. John Janick told *Billboard* in 2010, "Every song sounded like a smash. As soon as they walked out of the meeting, I said, 'We have to sign these guys.'"

The following year, Bruno ended up being a featured artist on those two particular songs, even though that wasn't part of the initial plan. As soon as B.o.B and Travie McCoy heard Bruno sing, they knew Bruno had to be on their recordings. "Nothin' on You" rose to Number One on *Billboard's* Hot 100 and "Billionaire" made it to Number Four. Bruno's dream of recording his own music was beginning to come true.

The route Bruno is going, he's definitely on his way to becoming the "Billionaire" he sings about with Travie McCoy.

In October 2010, Bruno finally released his very first album titled *Doo-Wops & Hooligans* with Elektra Records. All of the music was written by The Smeezingtons. Bruno said they gave the album this name because it has songs for both the ladies (the doo-wops) and the gentlemen (the hooligans). The album climbed to Number Three on the *Billboard* 200. In addition, two of the album's singles, "Just the Way You Are," and "Grenade," reached the Number One position on *Billboard's* Hot 100. "The Lazy Song," and "It Will Rain" also charted on the Top 10.

Bruno and his band—which includes his older brother Eric on the drums—are known for their retro style. They're often seen in colorful coats and skinny ties. And with

Bruno's trademark big hair and classic fedora, they look like they're straight out of the 1950s or 1960s. Their style sets them apart from other bands and really matches their unique flavor of music which blends reggae, pop, rock, R&B, hip hop, and soul.

Bruno started receiving award nominations in 2010, and the B.o.B record "Nothin' on You" won the Soul Train Award for Best Song. By 2011, he was winning awards on his own. He won two 2011 Teen Choice Awards for Male Summer Music Star and Breakout Artist. That same year, he won two MTV Europe Music Awards for Best New Artist and Best Push. He won a Grammy for Best Male Pop Vocal Performance and the Billboard Music Award, Top Radio Song for "Just the Way You Are." And he won the American

Bruno's band has a classy style all their own. Here they don matching retro suits: black shirts, black pants, shiny black shoes, gold jacket, and gold bow ties. They may look like they're straight out of the past, but their music and energy are right on par with the 21st century.

In the video for Bruno's "Lazy Song," Bruno dances around with a group of monkey-masked hooligans.

Music Award for Favorite Male Artist. In 2012, he won the People's Choice Award for Favorite Male Artist.

Bruno is definitely happy with how everything is going in his career. "Everything's good right now," he says. "It's really paying off because now my songs are on the radio. It took me a while to finally get it, but when I got it I think I got it right. And I'm very proud of how my songs are representing me as an artist," Bruno told *MidWeek* in 2010.

Success hasn't been easy for Bruno, though. He has definitely worked for everything he's gotten so far. Sometimes, he'll spend all night in the studio writing and recording songs. "He is a fanatic in the studio," Bruno's uncle John Valentine told the *Honolulu Star Advertiser*. He had visited Bruno for a few days in L.A. and saw how intensely he was focused on his music and his career. "The whole time I was there," he continues, "we didn't do anything—we just worked!"

Bruno also attributes a lot of his success to his family and upbringing. He said he's always been encouraged by his parents and he owes a lot to them. Bruno's father told *Hawaii News Now,* "I'm so proud of him, and I think he's really gonna go far."

In addition to writing, recording, and performing his music, Bruno also likes to help other people. When his band went on tour in the Philippines in 2011, his family joined them in Bernie's home country. While there, they visited an orphanage in the country's capital of Manila. This experience left such an impression on Bruno and his family that they decided to start a charitable organization called m.a.m.a earth that helps raise money for orphanages. In addition to their work with orphanages, m.a.m.a earth funds such organizations as Volunteers of America, Nourish the Children, Earth Schools, Positive Plate, the Grain Project, and Ashinaga to help with other important social issues. Their goal is to make the world a better place for everyone. Bruno's sister Jamie, who now goes by her middle name Kailani, runs the organization. Bruno helps to spread awareness about the charity. He also helps other worthy causes. In January 2012, he performed "Just the Way You Are" at the event "Hilarity for Charity," which benefited the Alzheimer's Association.

Bruno has big plans for his future. Right now, he wants to write more songs—both for his band and for other artists.

> *Success hasn't been easy for Bruno, though. He has definitely worked for everything he's gotten so far.*

Bruno often takes time out to help others. He performed with his band in January 2012 at the "Hilarity for Charity" benefit concert to raise funds for the Alzheimer's Association.

He knows this is just the beginning and he has a long, exciting career ahead of him. "I have so much more to go and so much more to show," he explained to the *Asian Journal.*

Down the road, he plans on returning to his roots and settling in Hawaii. He told Malika Dudley of *Hawaii News Now,* "My dream is to come back home and take care of my family. Once I do that, I'll be good."

1985	Born Peter Gene Hernandez on October 8th in Honolulu, Hawaii
1989	Begins performing with his family's band the Lovenotes
1990	Is featured on the February 14th cover of *MidWeek*, a weekly entertainment magazine in Hawaii
1992	Portrays "mini Elvis" in *Honeymoon in Vegas*
1998–2003	Spends teenage years performing with his band "The School Boys" and doing Michael Jackson impersonations on stage
2003	Graduates from President Theodore Roosevelt High School and leaves Hawaii for L.A. to make his way in the music industry
2004	Signs with Universal Motown
2005	Universal Motown releases Bruno from his contract
2006	Meets Philip Lawrence and forms The Smeezingtons production company
2008	The Smeezingtons co-write Flo Rida's "Right Round," which reaches Number One on *Billboard's* Hot 100
2010	Releases debut album in October, *Doo-Wops & Hooligans*; returns home to Hawaii on December 19th to a perform at a sold out concert at Honolulu's Neil S. Blaisdell Arena. Mayor officially names the day "Bruno Mars Day."
2011	Wins numerous awards including a Grammy for Best Male Pop Vocal Performance
2012	Receives the People's Choice Award for Favorite Male Artist

DISCOGRAPHY

2010 *Doo-Wops & Hooligans*

SINGLES

2010 "Just the Way You Are"

"Grenade"

2011 "Marry You"

"The Lazy Song"

"It Will Rain"

"Count on Me"

"Runaway Baby"

Singles as Featured Artist

2010 "Nothin' On You"

"Billionaire"

2011 "Lighters"

"Mirror"

"Young, Wild, & Free"

SELECTED AWARDS

2010 Soul Train Award: Song of the Year for "Nothin' on You"
(as featured artist)

2011 Teen Choice Award: Male Music Star of the Summer

Teen Choice Award: Breakout Artist

MTV Europe Music Award: Best New Act

MTV Europe Music Award: Best Push

Grammy Award: Best Male Pop Vocal Performance for
"Just the Way You Are"

Billboard Music Award: Top Radio Song for
"Just the Way You Are"

American Music Award: Favorite Male Pop or Rock Artist

The BRIT Award: International Male Solo Artist

2012 People's Choice Award: Favorite Male Artist

FURTHER READING

Lew, Debra. *The Bruno Mars Handbook: Everything You Need to Know about Bruno Mars.* Tebbo, 2011.

Tieck, Sarah. *Bruno Mars: Popular Singer & Songwriter.* Big Buddy Books, 2012.

Works Consulted

Berger, John. "Bruno Mars." *Honolulu Star Advertiser,* February 13, 2011. http://www.staradvertiser.com/features/ 20110213_bruno_mars.html?id=116103099

Berger, John. "'School Boys' in tune with doo wop." *Honolulu Star-Bulletin,* February 4, 2000. http://archives.starbulletin.com/ 2000/02/04/features/story2.html

"Bruno Mars and Phillip Lawrence." ASCAP, March 18, 2010. http://www.ascap.com/playback/2010/03/ACTION/ Mars_Lawrence.aspx

"Bruno Mars: The Fil-Am Artist with Universal Appeal." *Asian Journal,* January 5, 2011. http://www.asianjournal.com/ aj-magazine/midweek-mgzn/8386-bruno-mars-the-fil-am-artist-with-universal-appeal.html

Dudley, Malika. "Oahu's Bruno Mars on his way to music stardom." *Hawaii News Now,* May 12, 2010. http://www.hawaiinewsnow.com/Global/ story.asp?S=12463326&Call=Email&Format=HTML

Farber, Jim. "Bruno Mars follows his summer of hits with a big debut album 'Doo-Wops & Hooligans.' " *New York Daily News,* October 3, 2010. http://www.nydailynews.com/entertainment/ music-arts/bruno-mars-summer-hits-a-big-debut-album-doo-wops-hooligans-article-1.186181

Jones, Steve. "Bruno Mars' musical orbit seems inescapable." *USA TODAY,* January 25, 2011. http://www.usatoday.com/life/ music/news/2011-01-25-brunomars25_ST_N.htm

Lewis, Pete. "Bruno Mars: Out of this world." *Blues & Soul,* http://www.bluesandsoul.com/feature/593/ bruno_mars_out_of_this_world/

Lipshutz, Jason. "Bruno Mars Steps Into Spotlight on 'Doo-Wops & Hooligans.' " *Billboard,* October 4, 2012. http://www.billboard.com/features/bruno-mars-steps-into-spotlight-on-doo-wops-1004118815.story#/features/bruno-mars-steps-into-spotlight-on-doo-wops-1004118815.story

Moniz, Melissa. "Starring Bruno Mars." *Midweek,* April 14, 2010. http://www.midweek.com/content/story/midweek_coverstory/Bruno_Mars_Nothin_On_You/

Vozick-Levinson, Simon and Karen Valby. "Bruno Mars Triumph & Trouble." *Entertainment Weekly,* October 1, 2010, pp. 38–40.

Wete, Brad. "So who is Bruno Mars? A Q&A with the guy behind B.O.B's smash 'Nothin' On You.' " *Entertainment Weekly,* April 13, 2012. http://music-mix.ew.com/2010/04/13/bruno-mars-qa/

Wood, Mikael. "Bruno Mars Is Not Soft." *Village Voice,* August 18, 2010. http://www.villagevoice.com/2010-08-18/music/bruno-mars-is-not-soft/

Videos

Bruno Mars: Coming Home Documentary, http://www.youtube.com/watch?v=W0VfyQd_PhM

Bruno Mars concert live at the Neil S. Blaisdell Arena in Honolulu Hawaii, http://www.youtube.com/watch?v=6oyEmEayTrE

On the Internet

Bruno Mars Official Website http://www.brunomars.com/

m.a.m.a. earth http://4mamaearth.org/about-us/mamas-papas/